About the Book

Long-necked giraffes! European singing sensations! Waxworks! A 161-year-old woman! A 27-foot elephant! These were the wondrous spectacles P. T. Barnum entertained millions of people with.

P. T. always loved entertainment. As a boy he could listen to funny jokes or good stories for hours on end. No wonder he was considered the greatest showman of all time and his circus was called "The Greatest Show on Earth"!

Anne Edwards and Marylin Hafner fill this biography with many of the humorous and lively anecdotes so typical of the man himself.

P.T. BARNUM

BY ANNE EDWARDS

PICTURES BY
MARYLIN HAFNER

A SEE AND READ BIOGRAPHY

G. P. Putnam's Sons   New York

Text Copyright © 1977 by Anne Edwards
Illustrations Copyright © 1977 by Marylin Hafner
All rights reserved. Published simultaneously in
Canada by Longman Canada Limited, Toronto.
Printed in the United States of America
Edwards, Anne P.T. Barnum
(See and read biographies)
1. Barnum, Phineas Taylor, 1810-1891—Juvenile
literature. 2. Circus owners—United States—Biography
—Juvenile literature. [Barnum, Phineas Taylor, 1810-1891.
2. Circus owners] I. Hafner, Marylin. II. Title.
GV1811.B3E35   791.3'092'4 [B] [92]   76-52993
ISBN 0-399-61083-9 lib. bdg.

FOR

Rednaxela

It was a pity that Phineas Taylor Barnum was born in Bethel, Connecticut, on July 5, 1810. He would have delighted in being born on the Fourth of July. He arrived too late for the firecrackers and the parades that celebrated the thirty-fourth year of American Independence. He tried to make up for this all his life. He always loved spectacular entertainments and celebration.

Young Phineas was named after his grandfather. Old Phineas loved to make people laugh. One time young Phineas and his grandfather took a trip to New York. The voyage by boat usually took eight hours. But there was a great wind and the water was unusually rough. The trip lasted three days. Finally the boat approached New York on a Sunday afternoon. "The barbershops will be closed," moaned most of the fourteen men on board. They had grown unsightly beards during the journey. Old Phineas smiled. He had brought his own razor!

"I'll lend you my razor," he agreed. "But because the time is short each man can only shave half his face and pass the razor to the next. After everyone is finished then you can each shave the other side of your face."

Old Phineas was the first. After all, it was his razor. He shaved one side of his face and passed the razor on. When each man had completed his turn, the razor was handed to Old Phineas. He shaved the other side of his face. Then he leaned over the rail of

the boat to glance at the water. As if by accident the razor fell from his hand into the sea. How funny everyone looked with their half-shaven faces. All his life Phineas remembered how his grand-father's practical joke had made everyone laugh.

The young boy's father, Philo F. Barnum, was not a success at business. He was a tailor first, then a farmer, then a tavern-keeper, a livery-stable proprietor and then a country-store merchant. So he was happy to see that Phineas was a good student. Even at twelve Phineas was better at arithmetic than his teachers.

One evening Phineas' teacher

and a neighbor got him out of bed to settle a wager. The teacher had bet that Phineas could figure out a certain mathematics problem in five minutes. Phineas marked down the given facts on the stovepipe in the kitchen. He wrote

down the correct answer in less than two minutes, much to the delight of his proud mother and his teacher, and the astonishment of his neighbor.

His mother and father ran a country store. Phineas helped. But business wasn't very good. Phineas discovered that farmers were cheating his father. They would say they had ten pounds of corn or oats to sell and then only give nine. Phineas made them weigh all their goods in front of him. No one ever cheated his father again. But fewer farmers brought their goods to Barnum's country store.

Phineas didn't like to carry
sacks of grain. He didn't like to
sweep the floors or cut the fire-
wood. His father said he was
the laziest boy in town. But his
mother would argue that Phineas
was busy at "head work." She
was sure he would be rich and fa-

mous someday. Her husband had
to agree. The twelve-year-old boy
had already earned a good sum of
money on his own. He was working for the other store owners and
selling cherry rum to soldiers as
well!

Phineas did not like to work in his father's store. What he did like, though, were rainy days when business was slow. Six to twenty jolly, storytelling, joke-playing neighbors would gather around the store's old black stove. Phineas could listen to their stories and jokes for hours on end!

But later the store failed and his father bought a tavern. Then when Phineas was fifteen, his father died. Phineas had four younger brothers and sisters. Times became hard. His mother and younger brother went to work in the tavern. Phineas got a job at a general store in a town nearby. He

was paid six dollars a month and his board. Phineas had lots of ideas. He convinced his boss that it would help business to advertise. The store did well. And so did Phineas. He was given a good raise.

By the time he was seventeen, Phineas had saved quite a bit of money. He quit his job and went to New York. He wanted to start a business of his own. He opened a small tavern which was a success. Then he sold it for a nice profit. But his grandfather wrote Phineas to come back to Bethel. He was getting old and tired. He wanted Phineas to run his fruit-and-candy store. Phineas wasn't sure that was what he wanted to do. But he loved his grandfather and went back to help.

One day a man named Hachaliah came into the fruit-and-candy
store. He was a showman. As a
showman he found and presented
acts to the public for their entertainment. Phineas had never met
a showman before. He listened
with excitement as Hachaliah told
him stories of his life in show
business. Hachaliah had brought

the first elephant to the United
States. Most people had never
seen an elephant before, except
in picture books. He even built a
hotel in Somers, New York, which
he called the Elephant Hotel. A
golden elephant on a large stone
pillar stood in front of the build-
ing.

Phineas remained in Bethel another five years but he never forgot Hachaliah. He married a pretty woman named Charity and they had a daughter, Caroline. All the time Phineas was thinking about ways to entertain people. One cold winter day he said good-bye to Bethel and took his wife and daughter to New York. P. T. Barnum had decided to be a showman!

Phineas remembered Hachaliah's success with an elephant. He searched for something unusual to show as an attraction. He heard about a lady who was 161 years old. That made her the oldest woman alive. She swore she was present when George Washington was born and was his nurse.

Phineas rented an exhibition hall and handed out posters which told about her. People came by the hundreds to see her. They asked her questions about George Washington and about life in 1700. The oldest woman alive smoked a corncob pipe. Someone asked her how long she had smoked a pipe. "One hundred and twenty years," she answered.

P. T. had only been working a
year and he was already a huge
success. But many people thought
the old lady was a fake, a hum-
bug. Some even said she was
really made of india rubber,
whalebone, and hidden springs,
and that Phineas was a ventriloquist. This made people want to
come to see her even more. They
wanted to judge for themselves.

Phineas decided to take the old lady "on the road." He traveled to small towns all over America with her. Soon P. T. became partners with one of the first circus owners in America. For three months he learned all he could about running a traveling circus from this man. Then he decided to organize a circus of his own.

P. T. found a number of acts. He started a tour of the South. He traveled with horses and wagons and a small canvas tent. They would stop wherever P. T. thought the town was large enough. Then they would set up the tent and paste posters to the sides of buildings. He even hired a clown and a ventriloquist.

When P. T. returned to New York, he started his famous Barnum's American Museum. Before it had even opened, something mysterious happened during the night. Someone put billboards of wild and strange-looking animals on the walls outside the museum. Thousands of people flocked to the museum to see these beasts,

although Barnum himself had never said his museum had any wild animals. When they got inside, there were no strange beasts. But no one complained, because there were jugglers, educated dogs, rope dancers, giants, ventriloquists, and the first Punch and Judy show in America!

No one ever owned up to the
publicity stunt, and the museum
became New York's most popular
place of amusement. Families
brought their lunches and spent

the entire day at Barnum's. Some
even brought dinner. They
wanted to stay all day and night.
They had never seen anything
like this before!

P. T. always looked for new acts. He heard of a midget who was only twenty-five inches tall. His real name was Charles S. Stratton. P. T. decided to give him a new name. For days P. T. couldn't think of anything. Then he remembered the story of Tom Thumb, who was supposed to be a tiny knight at King Arthur's court. So P. T. named the smallest man in the world General Tom Thumb. Eighty thousand people came to Barnum's American Museum to see the little man. Then P. T. took the General on tour to England and Europe.

At that time there was a famous
singer in Europe named Jenny
Lind. She had such a beautiful
voice that people often called her
the Swedish Nightingale. P. T. decided to bring her to the United
States. Her fame was so great that
thirty thousand people came to
the dock to greet her. They

crowded on roofs to see her. They climbed on boats in the harbor to get a better view of her. The lovely Jenny Lind stepped down the gangplank. It was covered with a bright-red carpet. P. T. stepped out of his carriage and bowed low as he kissed her hand. "Welcome to P. T. Barnum's America," he said. Jenny could almost believe him.

The evening of her first concert came at last. Although the concert was to begin at eight, the doors were opened at five. The hall was blazing with gaslights. Jenny, in a beautiful white gown, stepped onto the stage. People wouldn't stop cheering. They threw flowers at her feet. Jenny didn't know

what to do. At last the crowd became silent. Jenny began to sing. When she finished, the audience shouted, "Barnum, Barnum!" The audience wanted to applaud the great showman who had brought them Jenny Lind. He had become the greatest showman in the world.

On April 10, 1871, Barnum opened "The Greatest Show on Earth." He put up the largest canvas tent ever seen. He had all kinds of animals and fantastic acts. Never had there been such a circus. There were waxworks, mechanical figures that breathed, Swiss bellringers, midgets, and giants. There was even a giraffe. No giraffe had ever lived longer than two years in America. Few people had ever seen this strange animal with its long neck.

The next year P. T. added a second ring to his circus. His Greatest Show on Earth was now the only one in the world with two rings. Then he found out someone else had added a second ring, so he added a third!

1876 was a special year for the Barnum circus. America was celebrating the hundredth anniversary of the Declaration of Independence. P. T. added many patriotic numbers. He added a Goddess of Liberty and a gigantic live American Eagle. People dressed as George Washington and all the Revolutionary heroes marched in a parade around the arena. There was even a chorus of three hundred singers. They sang "My Country 'Tis of Thee," while the Goddess of Liberty waved a huge flag!

Soon afterward P. T. met another great showman named
James Anthony Bailey. The two
men were quite different. Barnum
was more than six feet tall and
somewhat fat. Bailey was short

and thin. P. T. was always sure of himself. Bailey worried a lot. P. T. never did any physical work. Bailey liked to help the men who worked for him. P. T. liked to spend money. Bailey didn't.

But there was one thing the two agreed on. Together they would have a circus that no one could ever equal. So The Greatest Show on Earth became Barnum and Bailey's Greatest Show on Earth.

The greatest act Barnum and
Bailey ever had was Jumbo.
Jumbo was the largest elephant in
captivity. When Jumbo arrived in
New York Harbor, P. T. was at
the dock. Tears streamed down
P. T.'s face when he saw the twenty-

six-foot elephant. "Dear old Jumbo," he cried, and stroked the giant elephant's leg tenderly. It had not been easy to buy Jumbo. The zoo he had been in, in England had not wanted to sell him. But P. T. paid the huge sum of $30,000. Jumbo was now his.

Barnum and Bailey's Greatest Show on Earth was the success they had both dreamed of. But it was P. T. the audiences loved. He would enter the ring in his carriage. People would cheer wildly.

He was now an old man. His curly white hair circled a shiny bald head. He would shake hands with children and ask if they had had a good time.

P. T. traveled to London with the circus in 1889. A banquet was held in his honor at a grand hotel. He was the most famous American in Europe. Every afternoon and evening he would drive into the arena in an open carriage drawn by two fine horses. He

wore a frock coat and a shirt with an extraordinary number of ruffles and a big diamond in its center. He would stop the carriage from time to time, lift up his shiny black top hat, and call out, "I sup-

pose you've all come to see Barnum. Wa-al, I'm Barnum!" Men re-
moved their hats and ladies
waved their handkerchiefs.

P. T. died at the age of eighty in New York City. When he died he left a huge packing case in his office at the circus. An attached note explained that the contents were the property of all the men and women who had worked for him over the years. On the packing case in big black letters were written the words: NOT TO BE OPENED UNTIL THE DEATH OF

P. T. BARNUM. Everyone thought there was treasure inside. When it came time to open the box there was great excitement. There were hundreds of workers. Too many to fit into P. T.'s office. So they carried the box outside. Everyone crowded around the box to see

what was inside. When the top came off no one could believe what they saw. Books! Hundreds of books, all with a picture of P. T. on the cover. P. T. had left them each a copy of a book he had written: *The Life of P. T. Barnum Written by Himself.*

For a moment everyone just stood there. Then they began to laugh and laugh. P. T. would have been glad.

THE END!

About the Author

Anne Edwards was born in Port Chester, New York, and attended UCLA and Southern Methodist University. She began her career as a screen and television writer in Hollywood and moved to Europe in 1957, where she lived for fifteen years. Ms. Edwards is the author of numerous novels and works of nonfiction. She has written the Putnam book for children *The Great Houdini.*

About the Artist

Marylin Hafner studied at Pratt Institute and at the School of Visual Arts in New York. She has worked in many art-related fields, doing design and art for advertising, and designing textiles. She has illustrated many different kinds of children's books, including *Sunlight* and *Water Is Wet.*